Poetry

A
Tapestry
Of Words

Rona V Flynn

A
Tapestry
Of Words

Rona V Flynn

Index

Essence

There's an essence of me within these words,
woven through verse and tale.
It's not on the paper, it's not in the ink,
but hidden 'neath gossamer veil.

There's a spirit of me that's hidden there,
resting behind the line.
Unspoken from my soul to yours,
that which is utterly mine.

Rona V Flynn

A stroll along the shore

Is good for the soul.

At the Shore

Starlings, seagulls, wagging tails,
Tall ships with their billowed sails.
Bumblebees and butterflies,
Restful waters fall and rise.
Ice cream cones and flasks of tea,
Bag of chips, just sit and be.

Walkers, watchers, bikes and fun.
Playing till the day is done.
Strolling on the golden sands,
Passing lovers holding hands.
Watching sunsets, filled with awe ~
Best by far is Crosby shore.

Rona V Flynn

Time to put our scarves on!

Autumn Chills

Wild and windswept thinning tree
stands tall and sways outrageously.
Golden leaves are cast about
as autumn drives the summer out.
Nights grow darker, long and cold,
hedgehogs search for winter homes.
Hidden birds stay nestled tight
and autumn chills begin to bite.

Rona V Flynn

What an amazing sky
when the night is clear.

13ᵗʰ November 2017

Beautiful Moon

The full moon takes my breath away
suspended in the skies.
It causes me to stop and stare
in wonder and surprise.
Reflecting blushing sunsets
on glorious summer nights.
Serene and calm it rests aloft ~
A moon-watchers delight.

Rona V Flynn

Where there is love,
giving is the overflow of the heart.

Betrothed

Tis love to love, and heart to heart,
Be you together, or apart.
Tis holding hands and tenderness.
Tis giving all and taking less.
Tis knowing well and letting be.
Tis holding on, yet setting free.

Rona V Flynn

I've never forgotten the Bluebells growing
beneath my Grandmother's Lilac tree.
They still delight me and
my garden is now full of them.
Perhaps you have an early memory of
Bluebells too.

Bluebells

Bluebells 'neath the lilac tree
always captivated me.
Hidden treasure in the shade
moulded wholly perfectly.

Dainty petals curled and blue
with the merest violet hue.
Fragrant, sweetest scent sublime,
never bettered, hitherto.

Rona V Flynn

Bumblebees live differently to honey bees
and are gentle and non-aggressive.

Although males don't have pollen sacks
like the females,
their fluffy bodies trap pollen as they drink in the
nectar and vibrate their wings.

Bumblebees

Fluffy orange furry heads,
striped and fuzzy frames.
Yellow, orange, black or cream,
no two bees the same.

Hairy, gentle loveliness
buzzing round for hours,
searching through our gardens
for their Bumble-friendly flowers.

Pollen sacks are brimming
when they fly back to their nest
to share with other bumbles
and enjoy a well-earned rest.

Rona V Flynn

The meaning of life?
Now that's a big question...

I might need a bigger bar of chocolate
While I ponder...

Chocolate

Every day he sat right there,
all golden on the seventh stair.
Reluctantly I'd glance to where
he sat and wished the stair was bare.

As time passed by, I was aware ~
As he sat boldly on that stair ~
that I might feel inclined to dare
to reach for him in my despair.

Easter Sunday out of nowhere
made the bunny on the stair
bigger, brighter, gold and fair ~
He tempted me from everywhere.

I could hold back no more, I swear
the golden bunny on the stair
winked at me with *savoir faire.*
I could no longer leave him there.

I ripped the golden foil away
and ate his ears without delay,
and then the rest. It was the *best.*
Unbridled bliss. It made my day.

The moral of this little verse
is buying bunnies makes things worse
if you're trying not to eat *CHOCOLATE!*

Rona V Flynn

When I was a child,
a long cinder path ran alongside
the local cemetery, piggery and convent.
As well as collecting berries,
I walked it for many a year
travelling to and from school.

The Cinder Path

Crunching cinders 'neath my feet
I near the high black bars.
Wild grass spills through metal grills
with pitted age-old scars.

High walls now are beckoning,
my thorny prize is near.
Boughs adorned with fruit galore
finally appear.

Plump and soft and sweetly sour,
a feast for those who dare,
and as I rest to eat the best
the blackbird comes to share.

Brambles trailed our country lanes
for centuries long gone.
Nature's rich and lavish
larder, free for everyone.

Rona V Flynn

Confidence is most
Fragile

Confidence

Confidence is like a snowflake.
Exquisite, unique and delicate ~
Dissipating when it touches the ground.
Confidence is like a bubble.
Radiant, colourful and surprising ~
Yet the briefest touch makes it vanish.
Confidence is like a dandelion clock.
Intricate, complex and pleasing ~
Until the slightest breeze blows it to the winds.
Confidence is like a raindrop.
Soaring high, transparent and bright ~
Then dashed against the stone.
Confidence is sincere.
Vulnerable and fragile, it is filled with hope ~
Yet crushed by a whisper, shattered by a glance.

Rona V Flynn

A friend went to Uganda to help in an
orphanage.
He'd never liked dancing,
but while he was in Africa he found
a new way of being.

Dancing in The Dust

Dancing in the dust
in a haze of African heat.
Laughing and filling your soul with joy
with rhythms and the beat.

Dancing in the dust
in a place that makes you fly.
In a place that makes you laugh and love,
a place that makes you cry.

Dancing in the dust
in the sun's red evening glow.
Kicking your feet in the warm loose earth
and breathing the ebb and flow.

Dancing in the dust
where freedom tastes like wine.
Intoxicating to your soul
as dance and heart entwine.

Dancing in the dust
in a haze of African heat.
Laughing and filling your soul with joy
with the rhythms and the beat.

Dancing, Dancing in the dust.

Rona V Flynn

My Dubious Friend

I have a friend, forever there
on whom I can depend.
Be it day, or be it night
from start until the end.

This friend of mine will visit me
every single day.
Ever faithful, always true
in every single way.

My dearest friend I must embrace,
and intimately know.
for on this friend my life depends,
come sunshine, rain or snow.

My friend is ever-present
and will lead me day by day.
I have no choice but stay in step,
keep going, come what may.

Never will they pause to rest,
and never let me be.
For if I dally or daydream
they will not wait for me.

When come a day the end be near,
and memories slow unwind.
My constant friend will tarry not.
you see, my friend is Time.

Ever moving, ever present, never resting
…Time

Rona V Flynn

The wind can be as strong as an ox,
Or as gentle as a butterfly.

Free Spirit

It's gentle, soft and warm.
It's cutting, cruel and cold.
Straight as arrows it will fly
or swirl and whirl and fold.

It tiptoes through the grasses,
playing gently with the flowers.
It whips up waters high and wild,
it threatens and devours.

It's welcomed like a friend
or detested like a foe.
We don't know where it comes from
or where it's going to go.

It paints like Monet in the blue
and Turner in the grey,
Recreating heaven's canvas
every moment of the day.

Rona V Flynn

Don't you just love
frosty cobwebs!

Frost and Snow

Painted webs and woven silks
decorate the trees.
Their diamonds glisten in the sun
proclaiming winters freeze.

Silent snowflakes gently fall,
pure and pristine bright.
Shrouding all the eye can see,
they cloak the world in white.

Rona V Flynn

This blessing
relates to a beloved character in
The Silver Key who hails from Ibernia.

Gaelic Blessing

May there be blue sky up above you
and green pastures 'neath your feet,
as you wander by the river
through the thyme and meadowsweet.

Leis an spéir suas thuas tú
Agus féarach glas do do chosa
Mar wander tú in aice leis an abhainn
Tríd an thyme agus móinéir milis

Rona V Flynn

Giverny is the French village
Impressionist painter Claude Monet
chose to spend the rest of his life.
There, he created the beautiful gardens
made so famous by his paintings.

Giverny

Lily pads float gently
on the pond in Giverny
as sweeping willow branches
bow and whisper gracefully.

Muses of Japan
spill over through the garden flowers
and across the bridge of lilies,
where he painted, countless hours.

The shutters open wide to swathes
of rich and vibrant hue,
painted with the brush strokes
of a master with a view.

Though the house lies empty now,
bright yellows, blues and greens
flood the rooms with passion,
just as they had ever been.

And remnants of laughter
echo softly in the air,
of Monet in his garden
with the children playing there.

Rona V Flynn

Gossip and Lies

Gossip and lies.
It's no surprise
that always the wise
avoid gossip and lies.
For they recognise
there are no wheres or whys
that can ever give rise
to gossip and lies.

Rona V Flynn

Freedom to be yourself
in someone else's space
is a thing of beauty.

Inhabit Your Space

Inhabit your space
own it, it's yours.
Embrace your presence ~
Just *be*.
Leave space around you
where others can bide,
so they too can feel blessed
being free.

Rona V Flynn

Inspired by a coastal art installation
created by Antony Gormley,
Entitled 'Another Place'.

Iron Man

Looking out across the sea,
he sees the ships sail on.
I wonder what he's thinking,
Is he weeping when they've gone?
Does he yearn to see Another Place,
Australia or Japan?
Or maybe he just likes it her,
Our lovely Iron Man.

Rona V Flynn

Close relationships of all kinds
can bring pain.

So many families are fragmented
for so many reasons.
There is no other pain like it.

Jagged Edge

Discord brings the sharpest grief,
It twists the heart with no relief.
Our troubled breast craves peace and rest,
but chaos reigns beyond belief.

Discord has a jagged edge
which deepens to become a wedge.
Once there's a rift each side will drift,
creeping slow towards the ledge.

Rona V Flynn

Knight of Ludlow Castle

Tresses wrapped around her finger,
looking yonder she would linger.
Spying his blond mane, aflowing
in the breeze as he was going.

Taking breath, she could not utter
as her heart would fly and flutter.
Who was he, this gallant Knight,
galloping in robes so bright.

Every morn her mood would dither
as she peered far and hither,
seeking out his chiselled features ~
cheeks as rosy, fairest peaches.

"M'Lady." Maiden dashed unfettered.
"Do not fear and be not fretted
for I have a letter true,
on promise it be brought to you."

First she clasped it to her bosom,
Cheeks aflushed as spring's fair blossom.
Seal fast broken, words delivered,
Read again, she stood and quivered.

Pressing it with crimson kisses,
mind awash with countless wishes,
there she danced in love's delight
and joyful laughter for her Knight.

Twilight marked their secret meeting
by the ivy, fair but fleeting.
Tender kisses made her swoon
'neath the bright and wintry moon.

Close entwined they held so nearly,
'til they bade farewell so dearly.
Hearts surrendered to the other ~
Sweet abandoned to their lover.

Come each eve, they met with gladness.
Every parting ached with sadness.
Morn till night, she longed to hold him,
kiss his lips, and arms enfold him.

Then, alas, alone she waited ~
For her lover was belated.
All night long she tarried there,
for her Knight with flaxen hair.

Maiden pleaded with her Mistress.
"Come, be warmed … so pale, so listless.
Drink this hot wine, spiced and red.
Let me take you to your bed."

Gently whispering in her ear
She knelt and wiped her Lady's tear
but still all day she sat in sorrow,
through the night, and 'til the morrow.

"Please my Lady, take this potion,
it will help ease your devotion.
Though you fear your life must end,
time will heal, your heart will mend."

Soft, she touched her face so ashen,
dropped and wailed in morbid passion.
Cold as ice, her Lady stayed
still and quiet, in the shade.

Ivy threaded round her finger,
weaving slow where love did linger.
Ruby lips, now tinted blue,
kissed no more than morning dew.

Neath the ivy, pale and white
she lies fore'er ~ bereft of Knight.
Aching, longing, ever pleading.
Broken heart forever bleeding.

Still and cold with colours rent,
unheeding of the lark's lament,
facedown on the battlefield
lies her Knight, his fate full sealed.

In his pocket, damp and withered
rests her letter undelivered ~
Promising his quick returning
with undying love still burning.

Oft' on coldest winter's night
Beside the ivy when the moon is bright,
their forms appear embraced as one,
but for a moment ~ then they're gone.

Rona V Flynn

The Knight of Ludlow Castle
was inspired by a seat to the
rear of the castle itself.
It sits in a little nook surrounded
by overgrown foliage and ivy.

It's amazing
the things we get attached to.

Lament for an Old Friend

Of golden hue, both soft and true,
e'er ready to appease.
Of flimsy float, with, without coat,
'gainst gales or chilly breeze.

'Twas *always* my most favourite buy,
it washed and wore so well.
Until the day it blew away,
just *how*, I could not tell.

It was, no doubt, on my way out,
I grabbed it without care.
Then when I stretched, so as to fetch,
the back seat now was *bare!*

The wind was high, I tell no lie ~
I didn't even see
when off it flew to somewhere new
and slipped away from me.

Oh, to my cost, that time of loss
lays heavy now and then,
and I lament the way it went
ne'er to be seen again.

Elsewhere it lies, the wheres, the whys
Will ne'er bring it to me.
For someone else now loves it well
And I must set it free.

Rona V Flynn

People-time
is quality time.

Light Box

It used to be the Light Box
in the corner that transfixed.
Tomorrows World and Stingray,
Wagon Train and Take Your Pick.

The telly would enchant us,
entertain us and delight.
A cathode ray of sunshine
on a dark inclement night.

But now we have a new toy
to captivate our mind.
It steals our grace and kindness
and it makes us *people*-blind.

A glance across the tables,
reveals them every day.
Flashing screens demanding
they be looked at straight away.

Insidious, invasive
and intrusive, ever there.
Interrupting conversation
every which way, everywhere.

Let face-to-face enthral you
and eye-to-eye beguile.
Let heart and mind be present
with each other for a while.

Rona V Flynn

We're all a little quirky.
Each of us unique in many ways.

Loveliness of One

There stood a group of women.
It was difficult to know
if nature made them similar,
or *other* made them *so*.

Their lips were plump and rosy,
voluminous and wide.
Their teeth were bright and faultless,
defects all rectified.

Their noses were quite perfect
and turned up at the end.
All straight and neat and beautiful,
as is the current trend.

I saw a happy family
With ice cream at the coast.
They laughed and joked so freely
about who they looked like most.

Comparing facial features
and all kinds of quirky things,
they revelled in belonging
and the closeness that it brings.

They recognised uniqueness
and the loveliness of *One*.
Will we embrace our differences
or will they soon be gone?

Rona V Flynn

This poem was inspired by a sunny
Walk along the canal.
(Halsall, Lancashire, UK)

It was such a joy to see the
Meadowsweet growing along the banks.

Meadowsweet

Fragrant, creamy, fresh and dreamy.
Dizzy clouds of downy fleece
gather where the waters flow
and gently scatter mellow peace.

With scented balm, our hearts are soothed
and spirits touched with honeyed bliss,
surrendered to the heady scent
of Meadowsweet and its sweet kiss.

Rona V Flynn

The power of Music
defies explanation.

Music

When music touches our soul
its power makes time stand still.
Our spirit soars and we want more and more
of the joyous, ineffable thrill.

It resonates deep inside,
resounding to the core.
We beat as one with its baton
in rapt, abandoned awe.

When music moves our heart
to melancholic pain.
Tears will flow as we let go,
surrendered to the rain.

It fills us with delight
and lifts our spirit high.
Tis such an art that stirs our heart
in ways that mystify.

Rona V Flynn

Alan ~ 1948 - 2019

My Big Brother

My brother played snooker in our front room
and darts against our back door.
You could hear the thump of the bicycle pump
with his bike on the kitchen floor.
It was vibrant red with wide handlebars
and he made it from start to end.
But not from a kit, he took all the bits
from *scrap* as he'd nowt to spend.
With his chemistry sets and his magic acts,
entertainment was ever brill.
From his magical rope to his microscope,
and the acid jar on the sill.
His bike didn't cut the mustard for work
so he purchased the motorised sort.
With a rocket side-car it could really go far,
Twas the best thing he'd ever bought.
The next step up kept him warm and dry,
but was maybe a little bit tame.
He'd swapped his bike for a little red trike ~
Robin Reliant by name.
From his teddy boy hair, to his 70's vibe
when he sang as he played his guitar.
From his daring feats to sharing sweets,
He's my favourite (and only) brother by far.

Rona V Flynn

Our beautiful planet is struggling.
Together we can help by: –

Taking our rubbish home when we've been to the beach.
Recycling where possible.
Buying fewer single-use plastics (like bottled water)
Re-using glass jars for storage (great for the fridge)
Together,
the little things we do can make a big difference,

Plastic

Lapping waves weep bitter tears,
New islands are created.
Scrawny sea birds have their fill
with hunger never sated.

Enticing morsels dance and swirl,
entrapping aimlessly.
A starving whale gasps her last breath,
calves suckle desperately.

There was a time when creatures thrived
in this beautiful domain.
The waters gave them life not death,
will it ever be so again?

Teemed with shrouds of modern disease,
reaping destruction and pain.
Innocents sacrificed day by day
while the god of convenience reigns.

Rona V Flynn

Red Phone Box

Standing in the phone box,
she waits for it to ring.
The jingle makes her jangle,
almost dropping everything.

She lifts the black receiver,
says *Hello* expectantly.
On hearing his soft voice
she smiles and chats back happily.

Eating chips together
as they stroll around the park.
Holding hands along the way
and leaving before dark.

Kisses make them tingle
when it's time to say goodnight.
I'll ring at six tomorrow.
then the bus drives out of sight.

She lifts the phone on Wednesday,
they have the longest talk
then meet again on Friday
for another spring-time walk.

That's the way things used to be
before the techno-age.
No social-media messaging
to help us to engage.

No twenty-four hour access.
No texting *as and when*.
The phone box was the only means
of contact, way back then.

Rona V Flynn

Not so long ago,
Britain was full of Red Phone Boxes.

When I was young, it was unusual for people to have a
phone at home.
Calls from Phone Box to Phone Box
were fraught with difficulties ~
but as far as love was concerned,
I think it may have had its advantages.

Love the one you're with.

Roving Eye

Beware the man with a roving eye,
he watches when she passes by.
His heart is honed to heave and sigh ~
The man with a roving eye.

Rona V Flynn

Oh, those gorgeous leaves.

Russet and Gold

Beautiful Autumn,
breathe o'er your trees.
Weave your threads of golds and reds
with your chilly breeze.
Work your potent magic,
waft your sleeping brew.
Let all that thrived in summertime
surrender now to you.

Rona V Flynn

We can do
no more than embrace the
different shades of life,
as they carry us along.

Shifting Sands

Scrolls and folds, and greys and golds,
And shades of dark and light.
Whirls and curls as life unfurls
And weaves through day and night.

Greens and blues and sunny hues
Bring joys and pain our way.
Each day can bring such treasured things
To colour in the grey.

Oceans wide, the seas and tide
Forever ebb and flow,
And grains of sand forever shift
As waters come and go.

Meadows sweet, nature keeps
In breath-taking array.
With purples, yellows, blues and pink
To brighten up our way.

Life is all around us,
It beckons us to see
That only upon letting go
Will we be truly free.

Rona V Flynn

Take Care

Silver-Tongued.

We all know someone silver-tongued
with honeyed words aplenty.
They speak with such a kindly touch
but promises are empty.

Their eyes may sparkle like the sun
with every word that's spoken.
Our heart believes what it perceives
as someone warm and open.

But time will tell, and we will see
beyond the smooth veneer.
For when our mind is not so blind,
their *heart* is what we hear.

Rona V Flynn

So Much More

You don't know who I am,
I just occupy this space.
For what you see, this is not me,
I am *behind* the face.

You don't know of my mind,
my spirit or my core.
This is not *me*, this *shape* you see.
for there is so much more.

Rona V Flynn

A song of celebration for freedom and Spring.
From 'Star's Awakening'.

Spring

The river runs where'er it may
and waters wend along the way.
The birds are singing and preen and prance
while lovers hold hands and join the dance.

The daisies sway to the blackbird's song.
the trees are reaching high and strong.
Butterflies flashing wings unfold
and sweet bees make their honey, gold.

Rona V Flynn

Sometimes it is
the *tempest* that calms
the storm.

Stormy Seas

Sweet northern breath of Mersey,
stir up the rolling flow.
Toss the waves against the rocks,
whip up the sands below.

Lift my gloomy spirit,
blow the cobwebs free.
Set the world to rights again,
restore the harmony.

Rona V Flynn

Glorious Summer

Summer

The sun is high
The sky is blue
Breath of summer
Heartens me.
The trees are full
The grass is green
Breath of summer
Colours me.
The drinks are cool
The ice is cold
Breath of summer
Freshens me.
The stones are warm
The flowers are sweet
Breath of summer
Pleases me.
My feet are bare
The breeze is soft
Breath of summer
Pampers me.
The air is clear
The blackbird sings
Breath of summer
Gladdens me.

Rona V Flynn

Enticing
but deadly

Tasty Morsels of Woe

A drop of poison on the tip of the tongue,
bitter-sweet is the taste of decay.
In the darkest of night,
they will share with delight
tasty morsels of woe on the way.

Licking their lips, they will savour the words,
then impart them with such expertise.
and the hurt and the pain
of each link in the chain
will grow strong as they spread the disease.

Deftly depositing here and there
in the ear of those who will crave,
they will then share
to the pool of despair,
spreading grief that endures to the grave.

Rona V Flynn

The Artist

With specs on the end of her nose,
she empties out her swag.
Boxes, brushes, pencils, paints
spill from her Painting Bag.

Her folding chair is fixed with care,
she dons her crumpled hat,
then sits to view the sand and sea,
and folk round where she's sat.

She sketches fast and skilfully,
watching as they pass.
The yellow dress tossed to and fro
is captured, with the lass.

She steadies her red table
as she fills her water trough.
Her rosy cheeks are flushed with heat,
she takes her jacket off.

Images immortal
created on the page
where people stay forever young,
fated not to age.

She grabs her brushes briskly
and drops them in the box,
Folds up her chair and table
and grabs her painting blocks.

With jacket on, her work is done,
it's time for home and tea.
Another satisfying day
of painting by the sea.

Rona V Flynn

I watched my subject
while she watched hers.

The Collector

Boxes everywhere,
overflowing and piled high.
Collected for so many years,
from decades way gone by.

Different shapes and sizes,
dusty, heavy, dark and old.
With scents and ancient essences
and such enduring hold.

Sleep evaded often
and nights were sometimes slow.
They lingered always just in sight,
she couldn't let them go.

Although she didn't want them,
she held them close and tight,
Persistent, ever looming
they were blocking out the light.

Then began a change in her.
It's time to say goodbye.
She knew it was a challenge
but she looked them in the eye.

She gently sent them packing,
making each one history.
Slowly, and yet suddenly,
there now was room to *be*.

Without her dark collection,
space and light shone all around.
And even when she went to bed
relief at last was found.

We can live more freely
and it never is too late
to rid our minds of clutter,
and those memories we hate.

Rona V Flynn

We all have our clutter
in one form or another.
It's good to have a 'clear-out'.

Summer of seventy-six!

It was scorching hot, the sun cracked the flags,
we sweltered in the mid-day heat.
There were clear blue skies every single day
and everyone out in the street.

I wandered down to Lydiate Fayre,
No shoes and a long cool skirt.
By the time I'd reached the tables and stalls
those blisters really hurt.

Eggs were fried on the strangest things
for the novelty and fun.
Newspapers were full of it ~
The nation is out in the sun.

Don't waste the water! The government cried
and *Take your baths with a friend.*
A drought was declared, so parched was the earth
that we thought it would never end.

Flowers and leaves were crisp and brown,
we yearned for a cool fresh breeze.
Workers lunched round cool cascades,
the country was on its knees.

When the weather broke with a thunderstorm
And roads were washed and clean,
we heaved a heady sigh of relief.
Life returned to the way it had been.

Although countless years have passed
the memory stays fixed
and we recall with nostalgic fondness
The Summer of Seventy-Six.

Rona V Flynn

This was a summer that
Broke all UK records.

Life is full of
Amazing Coincidences.

Threads of Life

Our tapestry of life unfolds
with criss-cross paths and tales untold.
Until the future turns the key,
and looking back we clearly see.

Rona V Flynn

Touch

Each morning when her face is washed
and cheeks are soft and warm,
no soft caress will cradle them
or trace their perfect form.

Her hair is never ruffled
once the sleep is brushed away,
for no-one will disturb it
from the start to end of day.

When she passes by her mirror
and stops briefly just to peer,
no one shares her space to breathe
sweet nothings in her ear.

Her lips are only ever touched
routinely through the day.
No tender kisses linger there
to taste her sweet bouquet.

If she hurts her finger
and cries out suddenly
no other hand will reach for hers
to comfort tenderly.

When each day is finished
and she lays her head to sleep,
hers is the only breath she feels ~
her own warmth she will keep.

If she speaks into the darkness,
the silence seems to roar.
No loving touch sees out the night ~
just like the night before.

Rona V Flynn

The Power of Touch.

I almost called this poem Eleanor Rigby,
but these verses are not about loneliness.
They are about the importance of physical contact.
Lonely or not, single or not,
our body and soul cry out for touch from another.

A group of men find themselves on an
unexpected journey
with folk they barely know.
Without giving too much away,
this was a song they sang as they travelled
the country lanes together.
Adapted from a song in 'The Silver Key'.

Travelling

There's none better than a travelling band
Roving the hills together.
With the sailing white clouds o'er our heads
And fields of purple heather.
The cold winds blow and chill to the bone.
The hard rains fall and tall trees groan.
There's none better than a travelling band
Where friendships are forged forever.

Rona V Flynn

A large tree washed up onto the Beach.
The image moved, me –
This is the result.

Twenty-Eight Metres

Twenty-eight metres of worn out wood
once stood as a noble tree,
roots reaching down in the sodden ground
and leaves that were glory to see.

Twenty-eight metres travelled the seas
and rest on Crosby's shore.
Lying there with branches bare
where leaves will grow no more.

Twenty-eight metres of history
lay tossed by the sea and the foam.
Its tears are bathed by gentle waves
as it mourns and longs for home.

Rona V Flynn

Love!

Wedding Song

Tis the holiest of unities,
To find and wed your kindred soul.
The deepest love ye may e'er bear
Will cover ye and make ye whole.

The strongest love ye shall possess
Comes only from the deepest part.
To bare your soul in sacrifice,
To freely love and give your heart.

To share your tears of joys and grief,
To love with passion, sweet and true.
To know and hold their precious breath,
To sing love's song each day anew.

The strongest love ye shall possess
Comes only from the deepest part.
Bare your soul in sacrifice,
One for the other, one love, one heart.

Rona V Flynn

Look Beyond

What do you see?

The mistake ~ or the good intention?
The chaos ~ or the mind in turmoil?
The shape ~ or the person who holds it?
The mask ~ or the pain behind it?
What do you see?

Rona V Flynn

Those lovely long summer nights
quickly become a memory
when Autumn arrives

Where did Summer go?

Where did summer go!
The deep blue skies and warm sunrise,
the daisies and the butterflies.
Oh, *where* did summer go!

Where did summer go!
Sun no more from three or four,
we draw the blinds and lock the door.
Where did summer go!

Rona V Flynn

You Are Enough

It's not the way you speak
or clothes you choose to wear.
It's not your choice of perfume
or the colour of your hair.

It's not the way you hold yourself,
or contours of your face.
It's not the way you sit or stand,
nor how you fill your space.

Break free from expectations
of a world that asks too much.
Look inside, open your eyes
and *know* You Are Enough.

Rona V Flynn

Christmas

A time to remember what it's all about.
A time to get together with people we miss.
A time to include others.
A time to be grateful.
A time to love.

Christmas

It's not the way it's wrapped
and it's not the way it seems.
It's not the gift that's in the bag,
it's only what it means.

A heart that's filled with grace
is a heart that's filled with thought.
The only thing that matters is
the gift, not what was bought.

Rona V Flynn

Yesterday has gone,

Tomorrow is yet to come,

Today, live your life in the present...

Happy New Year

May your blessings be rich,
May you not shed a tear,
Lest the tears be of joy
and your love for those dear.

May you learn from the old
and look on to what's new,
breaking free of the things
that stop *you* being *you*.

Rona V Flynn

Tales

Of Wisdom

The Ordinary Penny

The disciple waited eagerly as the Great Counsellor prepared to give the days' lesson.

He made himself comfortable and began.
"There was an old man who lived frugally and wore ragged clothes. He was a kindly man and visited the temple every week, arriving early and choosing always to sit at the front. On this particular day, he had been sitting for some time, enjoying the calm and listening to the hushed voices as the temple filled.
Suddenly, he became aware of a man dressed in fine clothing, he was standing alongside him and smiling.
'Good Morning.' Said the old man cheerily, lifted that someone new was about to sit next to him. Alas, it was with crushed spirit that he soon realised his mistake.
"You are sitting in my chair." The well-dressed man continued to smile, waiting expectantly for the old man to move.

The old man was taken aback and took a moment to collect his thoughts. There were plenty of empty seats and he tried to think of a polite way of redirecting the rich man to one of them. However, he decided to graciously give up his place and moved along to the next one.
The rich man had many friends and he kept asking the old man to make room for them. Finally, the old man sat on the very last seat in the row.
'But where can I sit?' Came the plaintiff cry from another of the rich man's friends.
Now the Temple Master had been watching, and he indicated to the old man to give up his seat yet again. Having seen the consternation on the new arrival's face, the old man had already stood in readiness.

When he turned to see where *he* could sit, the old man saw only one seat was left, at the back of the temple, near the door. He moved quickly towards it – his heart pierced with disappointment and embarrassment.

The time came for the golden bowl to pass by and, as always, the poor man put a penny into it. He watched as the Temple Master removed it, tossing it into the Pauper's Box. The box never seemed to empty and he became concerned about the folk his coins could be helping."

The Great Counsellor paused and looked downcast.

"Sadly, the poor man died. When the village Elder summonsed the Temple Master with the news that he had been mentioned in the old man's will, he was bemused. *What can that poor old man offer me?* He thought, surprised that he had considered it necessary to make a will at all.
However, he visited the Elder as a matter of courtesy — *after all, he must keep face in the eyes of his temple-folk.*

As he sat down, he told the Elder he couldn't stay long, for he was *a busy man and had much to be getting on with.*
"Did you know the old man well?" The Elder asked him.
'I knew him very well.' He replied abruptly.
"Ah! Then you will know of his son?" The Elder held his gaze, awaiting his response.
'Son … he has a son you say?' The Temple Master seemed surprised and the Elder went on to explain…
"You see, the old man's son had recently made good fortune, but business advances required him to live in foreign lands. For the last two years he has sent his father four rare coins every month, to satisfy himself that he would live well. However, Temple Master, I'm sure you are aware that the old man led a simple life and did not desire possessions. This led him to set most of his coins aside, and as the bounty grew, he began to consider what he might do with them.

By now, the Temple Master was hanging onto every word. Excited to hear such thrilling news, he leaned in closer. *'Go on!'* He said, a sparkle in his eye.

The Elder shook his head and spoke. "I fear you may not have time to listen to the rest of my tale Temple Master. I know you are a busy man, and I do not want to keep you from your important business."

Straight away the Temple Master reassured him. *'But of course I have time. What are a few moments when I can stay here talking about my old friend!'*

The Elder smiled and stood, then left his table to retrieve the Temple Master's bequest."

The Wise Counsellor paused, smiling as his student eagerly waited for him to continue the tale.

"The Temple Master's eyes widened and his heart pounded as the Elder lifted a small, heavy chest onto the table. He reached in and withdrew a small leather purse, before pushing the chest to one side. After emptying the purse into his hand, he pushed a coin across the table to the Temple Master, then watched with interest. The Temple Master had recovered well from his belief that the chest was his inheritance, and enthusiastically seized the coin. He took it quickly to the window to examined it in the light. *'But it looks like an ordinary penny, have you given me the right one?'* He seemed confused and disappointed.

The Elder explained. "I have indeed given you the correct coin, Temple Master. The old man placed many rare pennies into the golden bowl. When he noticed the coins languishing in the Poor Box he decided to help you by distributing them himself. He felt certain of your approval, as you are a busy man. The rest of the rare coins are to be sold. The proceeds will buy homes for those in the village who have none, and food will be in good supply for empty tables. No-one in the village shall be in want."

The Elder thought it was a wonderful idea and told the Temple Master so.

The Temple Master grew red with rage and cut across the Elder's words. *Do I have a rare coin or not?'* He cried.

"You have a very ordinary penny, Temple Master." Was the Elder's reply - and the old man suggests that you put it into your Poor Box, as you already have everything you need."

The Wise Counsellor closed his eyes for a few moments.

The disciple enquired. "But what happened next, Great Counsellor, is that the end of the story?"
"It is indeed, daughter. Ponder awhile and tell me what you see."

The Great Counsellor lit the candle and they sat in quiet contemplation.

After some time, the disciple spoke.
"I see right away that the rich man was favoured because he appeared to have more wealth than the poor man. Perhaps the Temple Master expected him to be more generous when the golden bowl passed by?"
"What makes you think such a thing, child?"
"He knew the old man only ever put a penny into the golden bowl, and because he appeared to be poor the Temple Master looked no further than his ragged clothes."
"But child, he said he knew him well. Was it not the case that he called him his friend?"
"Then the Temple Master surely does not know the true meaning of the word 'Friend' for he knew nothing about the man – and would not the old man have shared his good news if he truly was his friend?"
"Indeed, my daughter – and what do you think would have happened if the old man's coins were not valuable?"
"I do not know, but a poor man who gives a penny out of his poverty gives more generously than a man with riches beyond measure."

The Great Counsellor smiled. "And what have you taken to your own heart from today's lesson?"

"Today's lesson reminds me not to judge by appearances, and not to show favouritism. It urges me also never to be too busy to show compassion towards those who sit alone."

"And what do you think happened next in the tale, child?"

"Perhaps the Temple Master threw his penny down and swept out in fury! But it is my hope that he took the penny with him – and went on to consider these things, as I have done."

The Great Counsellor extinguished the candle and looked at his disciple. "Your contemplation has been fruitful child – indeed you have shown yourself to be compassionate and insightful. These are qualities to be encouraged as you continue your journey to becoming a wise Counsellor."

Broken Treasure

The disciple sat down in anticipation of the days lesson.
The Great Counsellor made himself comfortable and began his tale.

"A Master and Mistress lived for a long time in a beautiful house. Flowers filled the gardens, and trees stood against the sky as far as the eye could see.
Sadly, all was not well as the Master was a cruel man in word and deed. For a long while, the Mistress had been keeping a secret box, and when she was in despair, she would conceal neatly folded scraps of paper inside it. Her sadness had been poured onto each one and the box was almost full. All hope seemed to be lost and she was sure her heart would break into a thousand pieces, before fading away completely.

~~~

One day her hidden heartache overflowed to a kindly neighbour who in turn comforted her, offering refuge while she searched for a new home of her own.
It was with gladness and relief that she took her secret box, along with a few possessions, and left the Master's house.

In good time, she felt strong enough to begin the search for her new home and it wasn't long before she was thanking her neighbour for her kindness and waving goodbye.

When she unpacked her few belongings, she placed the secret box beside her bed. Occasionally she would glance at it, never daring to open it to read what was written inside.

Three winters had passed when she finally ventured to hold three of the folded scraps in her hand. She ripped them into tiny pieces, took them outside and scattered them to the four winds, still unread. This she continued to do as and when her courage enabled her.

Three seasons later, she held the last few fragments in her palm, and when the winds finally carried them away a weight was lifted from her shoulders."

"But why did she take the box at all Great Counsellor? Could she not have left it behind, along with her wretched memories?"
"I will ask you this question in reply my son. If the box had held your broken heart, would you not have taken it also?"
"Then what can I learn from this tale? I do not understand."
"Let us sit and ponder awhile."

The Great Counsellor lit the candle and closed his eyes.

It was not until the candle had burned to its end, that the disciple was ready to share his contemplations.
"I have given much thought and to why the Mistress kept the box."

"Please explain."

"The box held many fragments, but every time the Mistress threw a few scraps to the wind, I think her heart healed a little bit more. It took many years to fill the secret box, so she had to find the strength to let those pieces go. I think I see now why she took it with her, for it was part of her, and part of her healing."

"Hurt leaves behind many scars, but if we choose wisely, those we spend time with can help to heal our wounds.

"Also, I was gladdened by her kindly neighbour. Her heart was filled with compassion for the Mistress when she shared her pain. Not only did she console her, but she offered to share her own home for a while."

"It is indeed a brave spirit who sets off to begin a new life. Now tell me, what have you taken for your own heart from this story my son?"

"I have learned that we never know when someone's heart is breaking, for her neighbour had no idea of the Mistress's despair. I realise also, that helping someone in their time of need may cause discomfort."

"You have used your time of contemplation well child and one day you will surely prove yourself to be a wise counsellor."

"But what became of the Mistress Great Counsellor?"
"Ah, the Mistress. She went on to live a life free from conflict, in a kindly dwelling filled with friendship and peace."

"I think she is enjoying her time with friends and those who are kind. My heart is gladdened to know that she found contentment, and a place where the secret box was no longer required."

"Indeed…"

Hearing is Believing

In the cool of the evening, the Great Counsellor sat beneath a tree with one of his disciples. They enjoyed the gentle breeze, watching with interest as people went about their business.

The Great Counsellor noticed his charge's eyes fixed on two figures talking together on the other side of the track. After a time, the young man's prolonged contemplation intrigued him and he followed his gaze once more.

"Tell me my son, why do you observe them so closely?"
"Well Master, I know they have had many complaints with a neighbour. I fear their tongues may be enmeshed in gossip because of the trouble the neighbour has caused."
"Pray tell me of your insight."
"They speak in hushed tones and their solemn faces are fixed in manner."
"I see."

The Great Counsellor sat quietly and waited.

Without turning away, the disciple leaned an ear towards the Master. "Perhaps I should break into their conversation to stop them?"
"And what then will you say?"
"I will hail them and wish them good eventide, then they will be on their way." A grin of gratification spread across the disciple's face.
"Bide a while my child – reconsider."

The Great Counsellor followed his disciple's gaze yet again to the huddled figures, then they sat in silence once more.

After a while, the Great Counsellor spoke. "What do you hear of their words, child?"

"I cannot hear them Master… but one of them turned to leave, then the other drew her near to continue their gossiping."

"It is such a beautiful evening, the birds are singing, the sun will soon be setting, and the sky is showing us the most beautiful of colours. Do you see them?"

The disciple did not reply.

Time had passed before he turned to the master. "I have given contemplation as you requested, and I believe I shall hail them."

"But what evidence do you have of their offence?"

"I have what I see and what I know."

"And what is it that you see, my son?"

"I see them talking, Master."

"And what is it that you know?"

"I know they are at odds with their neighbour."

The Great Counsellor sighed deep and long.

"Your insight deceives you my son, and for that which you do not know, you have missed the beauty that surrounds you."

The disciple looked bewildered as he turned at last to face the Great Counsellor.

"I know that of which they speak, and it is indeed a serious matter. However, it is serious only because it concerns one of the two, for she has a decision to make and the other endeavours to aid her in the making of it."

The disciple drew a sharp breath. "I did not know."

"This is true, for you know only a small part of the lives of others. But because of the little you did know, you presumed that which you thought was hidden from you."

The disciple hung his head. "I feel so foolish."

"Worry not my son, but use this opportunity to grow in wisdom."

As the Great Counsellor plucked some fruit, the disciple glanced across to the empty pathway.

"Eat and taste … look and see … hear and listen. Be present in what you *do* know and take pleasure in that which surrounds you."

The disciple nodded and smiled before taking a bite of the juicy fig.

Bathed in the glow of the evening sun, they watched it setting, enjoying the cool night air as the stars began to appear in the cloudless sky.

Because we know a fragment
of the life of another,
we must not presume to know
the whole.

I hope you enjoyed reading my book.
If you have a favourite poem
please let me know.

About the Author

You may already know a little about me after reading my poems, but here's more.

I love nature, my guitar sits against the wall half-way down my stairs, my watercolours don't get used as often as they should and I've loved taking photographs since my teens.

There, that's me in a nutshell.

Rona x

My second and third poetry books are now available.

A taste of Poetry Two reviews

.

Damsels and Dragons
"What a beautiful poem. So full of wonderful imagery. The process is pretty amazing and the author has captured the magic and mystery very descriptively." Nature Lover.
The British Dragonfly Society liked this poem so much that they shared it on their Facebook Page.

Blackbird
"The poem entitled 'Blackbird' is beautiful and I love the author's description of its song. It is such a magical sound and she expresses it so perfectly. I also like the blackbird's eye being 'starlight cloaked in ebony velvet.' Gorgeous!"
Lesley Rawlinson, Author.

Earth's Bones
"The author shows great insight into the Earth's amazing processes in the poem 'Earth's Bones'. I love it!"
Jennifer Jones, Earth Scientist and Author.

See overleaf for novels…

Also available on Amazon - Two stories with a touch of fantasy. (E-book and paperback)

Star's Awakening and The Silver Key feature the age-old struggle between good and evil, and the family's journey through it. The tales begin in Gawswood, a close-knit community with Star's family is at the heart of it.

Star's Awakening – Book One
Star's widowed father is the settle Elder. All is well, but as Star prepares for her coming of age, everything begins to change. Old enemies, the discovery of family secrets, and life-changing events lead us through their journey.

The Silver Key - Book Two
The continuation of *Star's Awakening* picks up the family's tale five years later. Life in Gawswood has been good - but all is not as it seems. We watch the human condition weaving its way through the trials and tribulations that beset them. Interesting new characters join them as they search for answers and closure.

You can find out more on my Facebook Author Page ~
it would be lovely to hear from you.

Printed in Great Britain
by Amazon

80898294R00075